MAKING
HEALTHY
F O O D
CHOICES

Food for Sports

Neil Morris

www.heinemann.co.uk/lib
Visit our website to find out more inf

To order:
☎ Phone 44 (0) 1865 888066
Send a fax to 44 (0) 1865 314091
Visit the Heinemann Bookshop at www.heinemann.co.uk/library to browse our catalogue and order online.

First published in Great Britain by Heinemann Library, Halley Court, Jordan Hill, Oxford OX2 8EJ, part of Harcourt Education.
Heinemann is a registered trademark of Harcourt Education Ltd.

© Harcourt Education Ltd 2006
First published in paperback in 2007
The moral right of the proprietor has been asserted.

All rights reserved. No part of this publication may be reproduced, stored in a retrieval system, or transmitted in any form or by any means, electronic, mechanical, photocopying, recording, or otherwise, without either the prior written permission of the publishers or a licence permitting restricted copying in the United Kingdom issued by the Copyright Licensing Agency Ltd, 90 Tottenham Court Road, London W1T 4LP (www.cla.co.uk).

Editorial: Andrew Farrow and
    Christine Mᶜ Cafferty
Design: David Poole and Geoff Ward
Illustrations: Geoff Ward
Picture Research: Melissa Allison and
    Maria Joannou
Production: Chloe Bloom

Originated by Chroma
Printed and bound in China by South China Printing Company

10 digit ISBN 0 431 11915 5 (hardback)
13 digit ISBN 978 0 431 11915 1
10 09 08 07 06
10 9 8 7 6 5 4 3 2 1

10 digit ISBN 0 431 11921 X (paperback)
13 digit ISBN 978 0 431 11921 2
11 10 09 08 07
10 9 8 7 6 5 4 3 2 1

British Library Cataloguing in Publication Data
Morris, Neil, 1946-
Food for sport. - (Making healthy food choices)
613.2
A full catalogue record for this book is available from the British Library.

Acknowledgements
The publishers would like to thank the following for permission to reproduce photographs:
Action Plus Images pp. 36 (Erik Isakson), 38 (Mark Shearman); Alamy Images p. 5 (Shotfile); Corbis pp. 4 (Olivier Prevosto), 13 (Wolfgang Rattay/Reuters), 15 (Joe McBride), 19 (Ron Boardman; Frank Lane Picture Agency), 25 (Reuters/ Will Burgess), 26 (Tim de Waele), 34 , 40 (Erich Schlegel/NewSport), 42 (Roger Ball), 51 top (Envision); Empics pp. 21 (AP Photo/ Paul Sakuma), 28 (PA/ RUI VIEIRA), 39 (PA/ Rebecca Naden), 45 (AP/ MARKUS SCHREIBER); Getty Images pp. 7 (Christian Fischer/Bongarts), 8 (Stone/Jed Share), 12 (AFP PHOTO/ FRANCK FIFE), 17 (Allsport Concepts), 18 (Photographer's Choice/GSO Images), 22 (Photodisc), 23 (Botanica), 33 (Clive Brunskill), 35 (Bob Martin), 43 (AFP PHOTO/ FRANCK FIFE), 46 (Doug Benc), 47 (Taxi/Ken Churnes), 49 (Taxi/ Tony Anderson); Harcourt Education Ltd pp. 48 (MM Studios), 51 bott (MM Studios); Photolibrary pp. 10 (Foodpix/ John E Kelly), 14 (Foodpix/ Michael Pohuski); Science Photo Library p. 24 (GUSTO PRODUCTIONS).

Cover photograph of Lance Armstrong reproduced with permission of Getty Images (AFP/Joel Saget)

The publishers would like to thank Rebecca Weeden for her assistance in the preparation of this book.

CONTENTS

Energy foods	4
Food groups	8
Carbohydrates	10
Protein	14
Fats	18
Vitamins and minerals	22
Fluids	26
Looking after your body	30
Training and competing	36
Health problems	44
Ideas for healthy eating	48
Recipes	50
Glossary	52
Finding out more	54
Index	56

Any words appearing in the text in bold, **like this**,
are explained in the glossary.

ENERGY FOODS !
– fuel for life ●

Most young people enjoy physical exercise in one form or another, and physical exercise is good for you. When you exercise, your body uses a lot of energy. This energy comes from the food you eat.

Food is energy for life. We use this energy all day, every day. When you run, jump, or take part in any kind of sporting activity, your body has to perform at a high level. Your lungs work harder to take in oxygen. Your heart beats faster to pump oxygen around the body in your blood. Most importantly, your muscles burn fuel faster as they work hard to help you move.

▲ Athletes use up a huge amount of energy in a short period of time. This top-level sprinter put everything into her race.

Variety and balance

The more active you are, the more energy you use, and, generally, the more food you need. However, it is important to remember that young people do not need a special **diet** to take part in their favourite sport or exercise. If you eat a healthy, **balanced diet**, your food should produce all the energy you need.

You might play a team game like soccer or hockey, or take up an individual sport such as cycling or running. If you take sport seriously and play for a school team or a club, you will know that it helps your performance to be fit. Part of keeping fit and healthy is making sure that you make the right choices about the food you eat and the fluids you drink. Food and drink provide us with the fuel we need for everything we do. Then you can enjoy your sport, which should be fun, at whatever level you play.

Eating sensibly and healthily is important even if you do not take part in competitive sport. Healthy eating is just as important for those who enjoy a kick-around in the park or a leisurely swim in the pool. We still need energy, and plenty of it.

▲ These players are taking a break from basketball to quench their thirst and replace lost fluids.

WHAT ELSE DOES FOOD DO FOR US?

As well as giving us energy, food does other jobs. It provides us with substances that help build, repair, and replace **tissues** in our bones, muscles, and **organs**. These substances are also needed to regulate your bodily processes and help make blood **cells**. They also help you to grow.

5

MEASURING ENERGY

Scientists usually measure the energy we get from food in units called **kilojoules** (**kJ**). Most sportspeople, and people trying to lose weight, use a different system of units, called **calories** (or cal). Since one calorie is a tiny amount of energy, people actually calculate in thousands of calories (called **kilocalories**, or kcal). To add to the confusion, they usually call these kilocalories "calories"! Most food labels give both measures of energy, but health books and magazine articles usually stick to calories. We will also use calories (kcal) in this book.

One kilocalorie is the same as about four kilojoules. To convert more precisely from one system to the other:
1 kcal (usually called a calorie) = 4.18 kJ or 1 kJ = 0.24 kcal.

The number of calories you need depends on many things, including your gender, height, weight, and fitness. It is also affected by how much energy you use up, so exercise and sports will influence what and how much you need to eat. The chart below gives an average for different ages, but note that figures may vary.

We all use up energy at different rates. Boys usually burn more calories than girls, because they generally have larger muscles that use more energy. Strenuous sports and activities use more energy than gentle ones.

Calorie burners	
activity (for 30 minutes)	**approximate calories (kcal) used**
judo	380
running	290
swimming	260
ice hockey	250
basketball	230
rowing machine	220
tennis	220
soccer	210
aerobics	200
jogging	200
cycling	190
badminton	180
golf	130
horseriding	130
weight-training	130
walking	110

How many calories (kcal) do you need per day?		
age	**girls/ women**	**boys/ men**
7–10	1740	1970
11–14	1845	2220
15–18	2110	2755
19–50	1940	2550

WOW!

If you ate nothing, your glycogen stores would only last about a day OR be enough to run about 32 kilometres (20 miles).

▲ Soccer players need a lot of energy. This is a women's international match between Germany and the United States.

STORAGE TANKS

We need energy reserves for all activities, including sports. Otherwise we would have to keep eating most of the time, at the same rate that we use energy up. In fact we have a number of energy stores in our bodies.

Some food is turned into a substance called **glycogen**. The glycogen is stored in the liver and in muscles. People with large muscles store more glycogen. If you have a low amount of glycogen, you will tire more easily when you are active in your sport. This energy store is the one that is the most readily available.

The largest store of energy is in the form of fat, which acts as the body's fuel reserve (see pages 18-21). Most fat is stored beneath the skin and around the body's internal organs.

FOOD GROUPS
– getting all you need

The substances in food that give us nourishment are called nutrients. They provide us with all the fuel we need to be active. Nutrients can be divided into two groups according to how much of them we need.

The nutrients we need in large amounts are called **macronutrients** and those in smaller amounts are **micronutrients**. The main macronutrients are **carbohydrates**, **protein**, and fats. They are contained in different quantities in all kinds of foods. Fats provide more energy than carbohydrates or proteins do. However, fats are not usually the best nutrients for sports and exercise (see pages 19–21).

▼ Food labels tell you everything you need to know about nutrients and other ingredients in food and drink. This makes it easy to compare different brands.

Macronutrients

The same weight of these three macronutrients provide different amounts of energy:

✔ fats provide 9 calories (kcal) per gram or 256.5 calories per ounce.

✔ carbohydrates provide 4 calories per gram or 114 calories per ounce.

✔ proteins provide 4 calories per gram or 114 calories per ounce.

Fats are therefore the most concentrated provider of energy, giving more than twice as much energy as either carbohydrate or protein.

The micronutrients are **vitamins** and **minerals**. We need only small amounts of these and they do not provide us with energy. However, they help us stay healthy and prevent illness. They are important to everyone, including all sportspeople. Without micronutrients you would not perform at your best.

There are two other essential substances in food – water and **fibre**. Water is an essential part of blood and so helps carry nutrients around the body. Fibre is important because it aids the process of **digestion** by helping the body pass faeces, or solid waste, easily.

A balanced diet

We can put foods into five main groups, based on what they contain. Like everyone else, athletes should eat more of the first two groups and less of the others.

✔ Bread, **cereal grains**, and potatoes, including rice and pasta: these starchy foods provide much carbohydrate and fibre. They should make up about a third of the food you eat.

✔ Fruit and vegetables: eat at least five portions every day. They give vitamins, fibre, and carbohydrates, and they should also make up about a third of your food.

✔ Milk and dairy products including soya alternatives, such as soya milk, for vegetarians: these are a good source of protein, vitamins, and **calcium**. We need moderate amounts of these foods.

✔ Meat, fish, and eggs, including beans, nuts, **lentils**, and other **pulses**: these foods contain much protein and minerals. However, you should eat them in moderation.

✔ Fat and sugar, including cakes, biscuits, crisps, and fizzy drinks. Fats and sugars have many calories and give lots of energy, but they have few nutrients. It is therefore not good to eat too much in this group.

CARBOHYDRATES
– the energy source

Carbohydrates are our most important source of energy. They provide fuel for the muscles, as well as for the brain. The basic unit of carbohydrates is a sugar called **glucose**. Glucose forms what are called simple carbohydrates, which are found in fruit. When many **molecules** of glucose join together, they form complex carbohydrates. These are found in starchy foods, such as bread and potatoes.

▲ There is a wide range of high-carbohydrate foods.

WOW!

The brain needs about 144 g (roughly 600 calories) of glucose a day to function properly. The brain relies on the bloodstream to deliver a constant supply.

Simple carbohydrates = sugars
There are five different common sugars:

✔ glucose, found in fruits and honey

✔ fructose, in fruit, vegetables, and honey

✔ lactose and galactose, in milk and dairy products

✔ sucrose, in sugar cane and sugar beet (making table sugar)

✔ maltose, in beer and malted foods (like some breakfast cereals).

Complex carbohydrates = starches
Starchy carbohydrates are found in bread, potatoes, pasta, rice, **maize**, **oats**, breakfast cereals, noodles, and **millet.** This is a group that should make up about a third of our diet.

FUEL IN THE BLOOD

The blood carries glucose from carbohydrates to all parts of our body, including our muscles. Extra glucose is stored in the liver and muscles in the form of glycogen, which can quickly be turned back into glucose when needed. This is how athletes get extra energy. When the level of sugar in the blood is low and muscles need more glucose, the liver turns glycogen back into glucose. This is why it is important for athletes to have high stores of glycogen before they take part in their sport.

People used to believe that simple carbohydrates (sugars) provided quick energy, while starches worked more slowly. However it is not as simple as that. Eating some starchy foods, such as bread and potatoes, also gives a quick rise in blood sugar level.

What do different foods contain?

100 g portion	carbo-hydrate (g)	protein (g)	fat (g)	fibre (g)	calories (kcal)
cornflakes	89.6	7.9	0.7	0.9	376
honey	82.4	0.3	0	0.2	304
brown rice	81.3	6.7	2.8	1.9	357
spaghetti	74.0	12.0	1.8	2.9	342
wholegrain bread	31.8	6.8	2.6	4.5	171
baked potato	31.0	3.9	0.2	2.7	136
banana	23.0	1.2	0.3	1.1	95
baked beans	15.1	4.8	0.6	3.5	81
apple	11.8	0.4	0.1	1.8	47
carrot	10.1	1.0	0.2	3.0	43
orange juice	8.8	0.5	0.1	0.1	36

PRE-MATCH SPUDS

French nutritionists heavily criticised the pre-match diet of the England players in Euro '96. Their menu of tomato soup, spaghetti bolognese and toast was said to be more likely to produce wind than a win. Potatoes, according to French scientists, make the best meal on the day of a game. […] According to one piece of research, a player should consume 200–300 grams of potatoes, boiled for 20 minutes, exactly three hours before going on the pitch.

From *BBC News* at bbcnews.com © bbc.co.uk, November 2004

GLYCAEMIC INDEX

Scientists have worked out what effect different foods have on blood-sugar levels. The **glycaemic index** (GI) gives a number to each food, showing how fast it affects sugar levels in your blood. High-GI foods, which raise your blood sugar level fast, have scores over 60. Moderate scores are 40–60. Low-GI foods have a score below 40. Sportspeople generally select low-GI foods before exercise, and high-GI foods during and after exercise.

GI scores of some foods

food	portion size	GI rating
white rice	180 g	87
baked potato	180 g, medium	85
cornflakes	30 g, small bowl	84
watermelon	200 g, one slice	72
white bread	38 g, large slice	70
muesli	50 g, small bowl	56
sweetcorn	85 g	55
banana	100 g	55
baked beans	205 g, small tin	48
macaroni pasta	230 g	45
pear	160 g	38
fruit yoghurt	150 g	33

Note that figures may vary depending on the exact food, its origin, and how it was produced. The figures are averages; GI ratings differ from person to person.

Endurance test

Swedish scientists tested athletes on diets that were low, moderate, and high in carbohydrates. They all had to ride exercise bikes at the same pedal speed for as long as they could without stopping.

✔ low-carb cyclists did 60 minutes

✔ moderate-carb cyclists did 115 minutes

✔ high-carb cyclists managed 170 minutes.

▶ A group of Tour de France cyclists tackle the hilly roads of the Pyrenees mountains.

TOUR DE FRANCE

The Tour de France cycle race is extremely demanding. Top professional cyclists cover around 3,600 kilometres (2,237 miles) in 21 stages, spread out over 3 weeks. The toughest stages include steep climbs in the Alps and Pyrenees mountains.

Tour de France riders take in about 6,000–7,000 calories a day. That is almost three times as much as an ordinary adult. They try to get about 70 per cent of their energy from carbohydrates, and spread the rest between proteins and fats. At breakfast and dinner, before and after the race, most riders eat lots of potatoes, rice, pasta, bread, fruit, and vegetables. They get protein from eggs, meat, and yoghurt, and fats from olive oil used for cooking, and from cheese.

▲ Lance Armstrong, wearing the yellow jersey of the race leader, wins a stage of the Tour de France in 2004.

Riders try to take in about 300–400 calories every hour when they are racing. They eat small sandwiches and energy bars, which they carry in a small bag. They top this up with sports drinks. All the riders take their eating and drinking very seriously. They know that it could win or lose them a stage, or even the tour.

Modern ideas about nutrition and fitness helped Lance Armstrong win the 2005 Tour de France at an average speed of 41.7 kilometres per hour (26 miles per hour). This was much faster than Maurice Garin of France, who won the first ever Tour in 1903 at a speed of 25.8 kph (16 mph). And in those days, cyclists were allowed several days' rest between stages.

PROTEIN
– the essential body builder

Protein makes up part of every cell in your body. Proteins build, maintain, and repair cells, and they are particularly important to growing children.

Proteins are large molecules made up of smaller chemicals called **amino acids**. When we eat proteins, they are broken down by digestion into acids. There are 20 different amino acids. Many of them can be made in the body from other substances, but nine of them have to be supplied in the food we eat. These are called essential amino acids.

Our cells are constantly being replaced, so protein needs to be taken in all the time. If there are not enough of the other two macronutrients (carbohydrates and fats), protein is also used to meet energy demands. Like carbohydrates and fats, protein cannot be stored for later use. If the body has more protein than it needs, the extra is broken down, and used for energy.

▲ Peanut butter is made by grinding roasted peanuts into a paste. It is high in protein.

▲ Snowboarders work their muscles hard and need to be very fit and strong.

Enzymes are made of protein. They speed up chemical reactions in the body, and without them the cells could not function properly. **Hormones**, which are usually also made of protein, act as chemical messengers and control many bodily processes. A good example is adrenaline, which prepares the body for action by making the heart pump faster and speeding up breathing. This hormone and many others are particularly important to athletes. They send more blood and oxygen to the muscles, and so improve performance.

MUSCLE POWER

Protein is important for building muscle tissue. This does not mean that the more protein you take in, the bigger and stronger your muscles will be. It is exercising them that makes your muscles larger. However, most sportspeople put their muscles under great strain. Because of this, they often suffer small muscle injuries during training and competition. Usually these are small tears in the muscle tissue. Proteins help repair these tears.

Most people in industrialized countries eat more protein than they need. Even top athletes should get enough protein from a normal balanced diet. Many experts believe that it is not necessary for them to eat extra protein. Young athletes should certainly stick to a normal balanced diet.

HIGH-PROTEIN FOODS

Plants make their own proteins from nutrients in the soil and water. Animals take proteins in when they eat plants, and their muscles are especially rich in essential amino acids. That is why meat is a good source of protein for humans.

Fish, milk, other dairy foods, and eggs are good sources, too. Vegetarians should make sure that they get enough protein by eating pulses, such as lentils, chickpeas, and other beans. **Tofu** and other soya products, as well as nuts, seeds, and milk, are also good protein sources. It is particularly good to eat high-protein foods that are low in fat. In the table of different foods, you can see that amounts of fat vary enormously.

What do different foods contain?

100 g portion	protein (g)	carbo-hydrate (g)	fat (g)	fibre (g)	calories (kcal)
beef steak, grilled	29.0	0	8.0	0	188
peanuts	25.6	12.5	46.0	6.2	563
salmon, cooked	25.5	0	4.4	0	149
cheddar cheese	25.4	1.4	33.6	0	407
dried lentils	24.0	48.8	1.9	8.9	297
cashew nuts	20.5	18.8	50.9	3.2	611
egg	12.5	0	10.8	0	151
spaghetti	12.0	74.0	1.8	2.9	342
cornflakes	7.9	89.6	0.7	0.9	376
wholegrain bread	6.8	31.8	2.6	4.5	171
brown rice	6.7	81.3	2.8	1.9	357
baked beans	4.8	15.1	0.6	3.5	81
milk, semi-skimmed	3.4	4.7	1.7	0	46

CASHEW NUTS

Britain's double Olympic gold medallist Kelly Holmes won gold in both the 800 and 1,500 metres races at the 2004 Athens Olympics. She claims that unsalted cashew nuts were a secret to her success when she munched on them to boost her powers of recovery between races. "All nuts are a rich source of dietary protein, which is needed to enhance the recovery of muscles after intense exercise," says Jeanette Crosland, a consultant **dietitian** to the British Olympic Association. "They also contain carbohydrate and essential minerals, such as potassium, that are lost in sweat, so they make a useful snack to replace those losses after a workout."

Copyright *Guardian Newspapers Limited*, 15 October 2005

STRENGTH AND POWER V. ENDURANCE

High protein levels are essential for sports that require a great deal of strength and power, as well as those that need great endurance. This is because both kinds of sports need high muscular fitness.

What is the difference between a "strength and power" sport and an "endurance" sport? Think of lifting weights. A person needs strength and power to lift a heavy weight, and endurance to lift a weight many times. Examples of strength/power sports are athletics (track and field), wrestling, gymnastics, rugby, and American football. Endurance sports are long-distance running, cycling, swimming, hockey, and soccer.

Be careful!

Most doctors and sports experts do not encourage young people to lift heavy weights or overdo strength/power or endurance sports. This is because their growing bodies may be more at risk of stresses and injuries. Always make sure that you are guided and helped by a qualified coach.

▼ Greco-Roman wrestlers use only their arms and upper bodies, not their legs, to grapple with their opponent. For Olympic competition, this power sport is divided into seven weight categories, from less than 55 kg (121 pounds) all the way up to 120 kg (264 pounds).

FATS
– essential for a balanced diet

Fats make up the third macronutrient, and they are also an essential part of a balanced diet. Some people think that fats are bad for them, because they are so high in calories, but we all need some fat in our diet, including **essential fatty acids**. Fat is needed both for energy, and to help our bodies absorb important vitamins.

Some fats are much better than others for all of us, including sportspeople. Fatty acids contain atoms of the **elements** carbon, hydrogen, and oxygen. Those with many hydrogen atoms are called **saturated fats**, and they are often called "bad fats". This is because eating a lot of saturated fats increases a person's risk of developing heart disease.

Fats with fewer hydrogen atoms are called **unsaturated fats** and are generally liquid. They are "good fats" because of a reduced risk of heart disease. A fat with one unsaturated fatty acid is called monounsaturated, and good sources include olive oil and rapeseed oil (sometimes called canola oil). Fats with more than one unsaturated fatty acid, such as sunflower and soya oil, are called polyunsaturated.

▲ Saturated fats are mostly solid at room temperature and include butter, hard cheese such as Cheddar, and fatty meat such as streaky bacon.

▲ The body stores fat in fat cells. These cells have been magnified over 500 times.

Omega-3 fatty acids are polyunsaturated fats found in oily fish. They are believed to help reduce the risk of heart disease. As you will see from the table on page 20, foods can contain different combinations of these fats.

BODY FAT IN SPORTS

Body fat is generally a disadvantage in sports. It makes athletes heavy and slows them down. Even when sportspeople are very heavy, a greater percentage of muscle is usually better than fat. People used to think that fat was an advantage in sports such as discus and hammer throwing, wrestling, and judo. In fact muscle is still more of an advantage than fat.

What do different foods contain?

100 g portion	total fat (g)	saturated fat (g)	monoun- saturated fat (g)	polyun- saturated fat (g)	calories (kcal)
olive oil	91.0	13.0	71.0	7.0	820
butter	80.0	52.0	20.7	2.7	747
cashew nuts	50.9	10.1	29.4	9.1	611
peanuts	46.0	8.7	22.0	13.0	563
cheddar cheese	33.6	21.4	9.6	1.1	407
grilled streaky bacon	26.8	9.8	11.5	3.7	337
avocado	19.3	2.5	12.0	2.6	190
lean minced beef	14.3	5.5	5.7	0.5	244
herring, cooked	12.4	2.8	5.1	2.9	216
egg	10.8	3.1	4.5	1.7	151

Fat choices

Different foods vary greatly in their levels of saturated fat. Of the top five in the list above, the percentages of saturates in the total fat are:

✔ butter 65%

✔ cheddar cheese 64%

✔ cashew nuts 20%

✔ peanuts 19%

✔ olive oil 14%

Some other cheeses have less saturated fat than cheddar. Italian mozzarella cheese, for example, has little over half the saturated fat content of cheddar. Many cooks choose to use olive oil rather than other fats, such as butter, for cooking, because olive oil contains much less saturated fat.

EXCEPTIONAL SUMO

The ancient Japanese sport of sumo wrestling is the exception as far as body fat is concerned. This may be partly because of tradition, but fat does give a real advantage. This is because the object of the sport is to push the opponent out of the ring or make him touch the floor with any part of his body except the soles of his feet. Speed and agility can be important, but the heavier wrestler usually wins.

Top sumo wrestlers have strong muscles, but it is most important for them to have lots of fat around the belly and hips. This lowers their centre of gravity and makes it much harder to push them off balance. They train to be heavy and may reach a weight of up to 265 kg (584 pounds). That is more than three times heavier than an average adult man.

▲ Asashoryu Akinori was the first Mongolian wrestler to reach the highest sumo rank. Here he performs a ceremony before a bout of wrestling.

CHUNKY *CHANKO*

Chanko, the traditional dish of sumo wrestlers, is a hearty stew with meat or seafood and vegetables. During sumo tournaments most wrestlers eat the chicken version, because they believe that chickens bring good luck – they walk on two legs, which is how the wrestlers want to remain. Salt is also thought of as a good thing. Before a bout, wrestlers usually scatter a handful of salt in the ring, to guard against evil spirits and injuries.

Some typical *chanko* ingredients are: chicken, potatoes, egg noodles, onions, carrots, leeks, radishes, mushrooms, cabbage, deep-fried tofu, soy sauce, sweet rice wine, and salt. Wrestlers eat large amounts to put on weight. The ingredients are not particularly fatty, but they contain a huge number of calories, so the body stores the excess as fat. Many wrestlers sleep for several hours after eating an enormous meal.

VITAMINS AND MINERALS
– a little goes a long way

Vitamins and minerals are called micronutrients because we need so little of them. Tiny quantities are enough, but they are still essential. Vitamins and minerals do not provide us with energy, but they help the body use food properly and so affect our energy levels.

Vitamins are chemical compounds that are found in plants, animals, some yeasts, and bacteria. There are at least 13 vitamins. They are sometimes known by their chemical names and also by letter codes (thiamin and B1 are the same vitamin, for example). Vitamins are vitally important because they regulate the chemical reactions used by the body to convert food into energy. Vitamins B and C are soluble (dissolve) in water and the body cannot store them. We need a constant supply of these vitamins from our food.

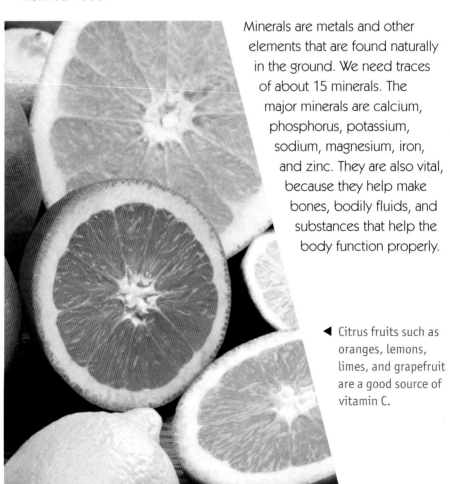

Minerals are metals and other elements that are found naturally in the ground. We need traces of about 15 minerals. The major minerals are calcium, phosphorus, potassium, sodium, magnesium, iron, and zinc. They are also vital, because they help make bones, bodily fluids, and substances that help the body function properly.

◀ Citrus fruits such as oranges, lemons, limes, and grapefruit are a good source of vitamin C.

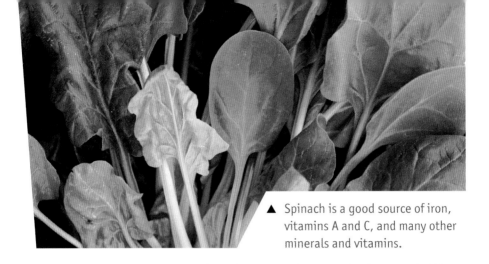

▲ Spinach is a good source of iron, vitamins A and C, and many other minerals and vitamins.

What do different foods contain?

100 g portion	vitamin B 1 (mg)	vitamin C (mg)	calcium (mg)	iron (mg)
apple	0.03	6.0	4	0.1
banana	0.05	9.1	6	0.3
baked beans	0.09	0	53	1.4
beef, minced	0.05	0	18	3.1
cabbage	0.15	49.0	52	0:7
cheddar cheese	0.03	0	720	0.3
cornflakes	1.00	0	15	6.7
milk	0.03	1.0	115	0.06
sardines, tinned	0.04	0	550	2.9
spaghetti, boiled	0.01	0	7	0.5
white bread	0.21	0	110	1.6

These are tiny amounts of vitamins and minerals. One milligram (mg) is one thousandth of a gram.

Especially for athletes

These four substances are particularly useful in the following ways:

✔ Vitamin B 1 (thiamin) is found in vegetables, pulses, nuts, meat, and **whole grains**. It helps the body release energy from carbohydrates in food.

✔ Vitamin C, also called ascorbic acid, is found in fruit and vegetables. It helps build healthy blood vessels, bones, and gums. It also helps to produce collagen, a substance that holds tissues together.

✔ Calcium is found in most foods, and especially in milk and dairy products. It is essential for building strong bones, and helps muscles work well.

✔ Iron is plentiful in meat, spinach, pulses, dried fruit, and sardines. It is essential for helping to form the different substances that carry oxygen in the blood and in muscle cells.

Eating a balanced diet is the best way to obtain enough of these vitamins.

VITAMIN AND MINERAL SUPPLEMENTS

Many sportspeople take extra vitamins and minerals in the form of tablets. Some believe that these **supplements** improve both their health and their performance. There have been many studies to try to prove this one way or the other. Most studies have shown that supplements really only help athletes who are very low on a particular vitamin or mineral. If this is the case, the person should be seen by a doctor.

There is often a big difference between what people believe and real scientific evidence. Some of the studies quoted by the companies that sell supplements may not have been very thorough. Some top sportspeople may believe in certain substances because they think they have worked wonders for them. This may not really be the case.

Too much can sometimes be a bad thing. For example, too much vitamin A can cause nausea and even liver damage. Too much vitamin D can result in high blood pressure or kidney problems.

If you have a good, balanced diet, you will be getting all the minerals and vitamins you need – as well as all the nutrients. You will not need any supplements. These should never be taken without consulting a medical expert.

Some sports scientists recommend that adult sportspeople take extra magnesium or calcium, since both are important minerals for the function of muscles. However, unless the player has a deficiency in either mineral, the supplements will not make much difference. Some athletes believe that chromium tablets can help them burn off fat.

◀ Fish-oil capsules contain omega-3 fatty acids (see page 19) and vitamin E.

Others believe chromium can help build extra muscle. Yet research has shown that the tablets do not help. It has even been suggested that too much chromium can cause problems.

Leg cramps and muscular pain are very common in all sports, because of the strain put on muscles. Americans call a sharp pain a "charley horse", which is thought to be a baseball term dating from the 1880s. It may have come from a player's name, or even the name of a groundsman's horse! Many sportspeople used to take salt tablets, thinking that they helped against cramp and other muscle problems. Salt supplements can irritate the stomach and cause people to feel sick and even vomit.

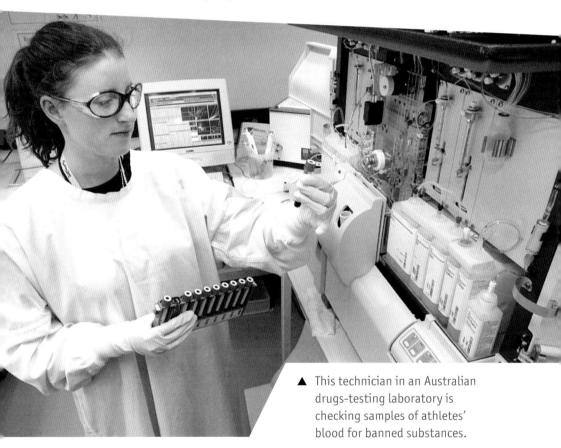

▲ This technician in an Australian drugs-testing laboratory is checking samples of athletes' blood for banned substances.

BANNED SUBSTANCES

Sports ban the use of performance-enhancing drugs such as steroids. There have been some cases where athletes who have failed drugs tests claim that the results were caused by legal dietary supplements bought in a chemist or health-food store. This is possible, but most sports authorities take a tough line. Top sportspeople need to be very careful about what they add to their diet.

FLUIDS
– vital to our health

Did you know that you can survive much longer without food than without water? Water is vital to our health. It is an essential part of blood and so helps carry nutrients around the body. It is needed for the breakdown of energy. Water also makes up **urine**, which helps to take waste products from the body.

The reason we have to drink a lot is because we need to replace the water that our body uses all the time. In hot weather you need to drink more, because the body loses so much through sweating. This is why drinking is so important to sportspeople. About three quarters of the energy put into exercise is turned into heat. An athlete may produce 20 calories (kcal) of heat energy every minute, and this has to be removed from the body.

▼ This cyclist has been sweating a great deal during his race. He needs to drink a lot to replace lost fluids.

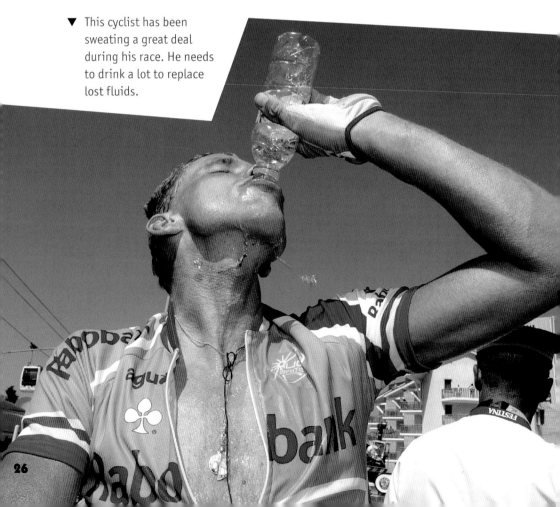

That is why sport is a sweaty business. Water from your body is carried to your skin as sweat, where it evaporates so that you lose heat. The harder you exercise, the hotter you get and the more you sweat. The more you sweat, the more you need to drink to replace the water.

During exercise an average sportsperson might use up around 1 litre (2 pints) of fluid. A serious marathon runner might lose twice as much as that on a hot day. The amounts vary according to the athlete's size, weight, and fitness.

HOW MUCH WATER?

Most people need about 6–8 glasses, or 1.2 litres (2.5 pints), of fluid a day, plus however much they lose during exercise. The most important thing is to make sure that you are well **hydrated** before exercise. This means drinking plenty of fluid before the event. Then add an extra 150 ml (5 fluid ounces) or more just before you start.

During exercise try to drink small amounts frequently - about 150 ml (5 fluid ounces) every 15 minutes or so. After exercise, drink plenty immediately and carry on until you are no longer thirsty.

THE WENGER DIET

Arsenal manager, Arsene Wenger, is known for his scientific approach to feeding his team. When he first came to the club in 1996, he immediately altered the players' dinner menus. Sugar, red meat, chips, fried foods, and dairy products were out. Vegetables, fish, chicken and plenty of water were definitely in. Arsene goes even further and uses a "pee chart" to measure the level of hydration of his players. Their first pee of the day is measured against a colour chart to make sure they are drinking enough water.

From *BBC News* at bbcnews.com © bbc.co.uk, November 2004

Pee charts

Pee charts are small laminated cards with eight colour strips on them. The idea is for a sportsperson to compare the colour of their urine with the chart.

✔ If it is similar to numbers 1–3 (shades of very pale yellow), the player is fine.

✔ The yellow colour of numbers 4 and 5 mean that the player is dehydrated.

✔ Numbers 6–8 (dark yellow to light brown) show severe dehydration.

DEHYDRATION

Dehydration is a major problem for any athlete. If you are dehydrated, you will suddenly feel weak and dizzy. You may also suffer from cramp and feel a headache coming on. It is essential to cool down and drink as quickly as possible.

Dehydration is not only a problem in warm climates. It can happen when you are skiing or snowboarding, too. The dry, cold air of the mountains also has an effect. As you glide down the mountain, you are losing water through your breath as well as your sweat. However, the cold reduces your sensation of thirst, which makes the problem worse. Skiing instructors encourage everyone to drink lots.

In a scientific study, runners ran a long-distance race twice under the same conditions on different occasions. The first time they drank their usual amount, but on the other occasion they were purposely slightly dehydrated. Their times suffered by 7 per cent – more than 2 minutes over 10,000 metres (6.2 miles).

▼ A soccer player celebrates victory with a sports drink.

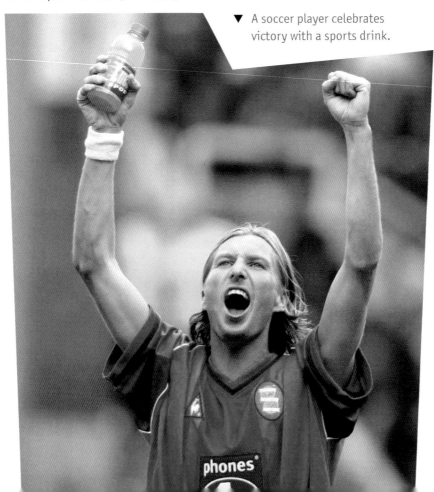

ALCOHOL AND DEHYDRATION

Alcoholic drinks, such as beer, wine, and spirits, make people want to urinate more. This means that alcohol can quickly cause dehydration. It also reduces coordination and decreases reaction time. Drinking alcohol can also lead to a wide range of health problems, and young people should avoid it.

SPORTS DRINKS

You have probably seen these advertised. You may also have noticed that sports stars usually have their own individual drinks or take a special sports drink. Some people may think that this is all just advertising and an attempt to sell more products, but sports drinks really do work.

They contain carbohydrate (usually in the form of glucose, which is a type of sugar) to provide energy. They also contain **electrolytes**, which help control fluid balance in the body. Sports drinks are absorbed into the body faster than water. They also make you want to drink more. Some sports drinks have added vitamins, as well as flavourings, colours, and additives. Drinking water is still the best way to rehydrate, but sports drinks can also help, and provide extra energy.

What's the difference?

There are three different kinds of sports drinks.

✔ *Isotonic drinks* contain about the same concentration of carbohydrates and electrolytes as the body's own fluids (4–8 grams carbohydrate per 100 millilitres of fluid).

✔ *Hypotonic drinks* contain a lower concentration (less than 4 g/100 ml); these are absorbed faster than water but do not contribute much energy.

✔ *Hypertonic drinks* have a higher concentration (more than 8 g/100 ml); these are absorbed more slowly than water.

OVERHYDRATION

Some sportspeople who compete in endurance events such as triathlons can suffer from overhydration. That happens when they take in lots of water but not enough electrolytes to replace the ones lost. Some signs of overhydration include confusion, disorientation, and nausea. Sports drinks help you avoid having too much water in your system and not enough of the natural salts your body needs.

LOOKING AFTER YOUR BODY
– it's the only one you've got

Our bodies are not all the same shape, but we can all take part in sport. No matter what your shape, if you are well, you can enjoy exercise and sports. That exercise will then get you fit and keep you feeling well!

Scientists divide people into three basic body shapes, though most of us combine some of these characteristics. The three types are:

- ectomorph – thin and delicate
- mesomorph – compact and muscular
- endomorph – round with more body fat.

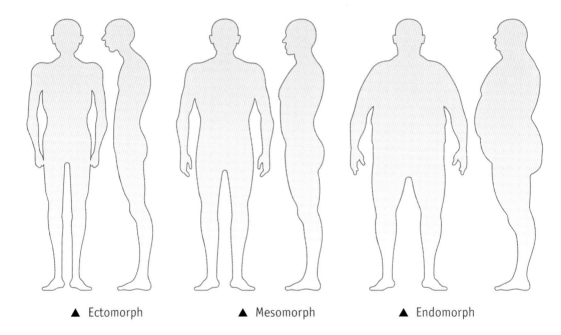

▲ Ectomorph   ▲ Mesomorph   ▲ Endomorph

Most successful sportspeople are in the medium mesomorph range. That's because they have a good combination of the two main bodily elements – lean body tissue (including muscle) and body fat. Muscles are obviously useful in any sport, but fat seldom helps performance.

THE BODY MASS INDEX

Scientists have worked out ways to help people check that they are the right weight. The best-known is the Body Mass Index (BMI). This compares a person's weight to their height. There is no ideal weight, but there is a healthy range. The BMI was developed in 1846 by a Belgian mathematician and astronomer, Adolphe Quetelet (1796–1874). It is still sometimes called the Quetelet Index.

The BMI is simply a guide, and it is intended for healthy adults. It is not suitable for younger people, who are still growing and whose bodies are still developing.

An adult person's BMI is calculated by dividing their weight (in kilograms) by the square of their height (in metres). This results in a figure, which can be compared with this scale:

✔ less than 17.5 = underweight

✔ 17.5–24.9 = fine

✔ 25–29.9 = overweight

✔ 30+ = obese

A person who is 1.6 metres (5.2 feet) tall and weighs 55 kilograms (120 pounds) has a BMI of 21.5. This falls within the normal range. There are many calculators on the Internet that you can use to calculate your BMI.

Athletes with very well-developed muscles often find that they fall into the overweight category on BMI and other tests. This can be misleading, because they probably have a healthy body shape with very little fat.

Adult sportsmen and sportswomen can undergo other tests to check their body composition and especially their fat distribution. This includes using callipers, which are like a large pair of tweezers, to measure the layer of fat on the body's surface. They do this to make sure that their body is allowing them to perform at their best.

APPLES AND PEARS

People who have too much weight around their middle are said to have an "apple" shape. They have excess fat stored in the stomach area, and this may increase their risk of developing heart disease and diabetes. If their weight is mainly around the hips and bottom, they have what is called a "pear" shape. This is generally healthier.

FLUCTUATING WEIGHT

A person's weight does not stay the same all the time. Small losses or gains are perfectly normal. A healthy adult might fluctuate by up to 2 kilograms (4.4 pounds) a day.

If you think you are overweight, do not just go on a weight-losing diet. You should only do this under the supervision of a qualified health specialist. It's more important to stick to a balanced diet. At the same time it is good to cut down on sweet foods, such as cakes and fizzy drinks, as well as fatty foods such as burgers, fry-ups, and chips.

SHORT, LIGHT, AND STRONG

Gymnastics is one of the oldest sports in the world. It was popular in ancient Greece, where it was used as a way of training young men to be fit for battle. The modern form of the sport began in the early 19th century in Sweden, and it soon spread to Germany and other countries.

WOW!

In the first modern Olympic Games, which took place in Athens in 1896, there were eight men's events. One of these was rope-climbing. This was judged on the time it took to get to the top.

Top gymnasts are generally short and light. Yet they have to be amazingly strong and have great explosive power. They also need both balance and flexibility.

Top gymnasts tend to be young compared to other sportspeople. Romanian gymnast Nadia Comaneci was just 14 years old when she won three Olympic gold medals in 1976. Her achievements included the first ever perfect score of 10 in an Olympic gymnastic event (and she scored seven of them!). At the 2004 Olympics in Athens, the women's all-round winner was the American gymnast Carly Patterson, who was aged 16 and was 1.45 metres (4 feet 9 inches) tall.

Gymnasts need to be very fit and healthy, so that they can put in long hours of hard practice. Carly Patterson, for example, trained for up to 35 hours every week. That is an average of 7 hours a day, 5 days a week!

Young people who take up gymnastics become very aware of the way their body looks. This is because it is an aesthetic sport, which means that the beauty of their movements is important. Their performance is scored by a team of judges, who watch the gymnasts very carefully.

BODY IMAGE

Many young female gymnasts work hard to be thin. There is a danger that they might not eat enough nutritious food. This can lead to problems and eating disorders (see page 45). Research at American universities shows that many female gymnasts want to lose weight and be thinner. Yet many young male gymnasts want to build up their muscles and put on weight.

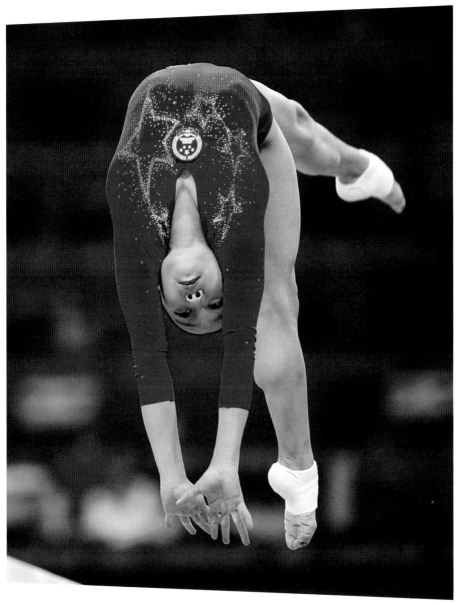

▲ Chinese gymnast Li Ya shows amazing elegance and athleticism on the balance beam. The wooden beam is just 10 cm (3.9 inches) wide and stands 1.2 m (3.9 feet) off the floor.

VEGETARIAN ATHLETES

Vegetarians are people who do not eat meat. Some eat fish or seafood, and many are happy to eat a few animal products, such as milk, cheese, and eggs. Vegans do not eat any foods of animal origin, including all dairy products and honey (which is made by bees).

Nutritionists agree that a vegetarian diet can be perfectly healthy. Meat contains a lot of protein, so vegetarians and vegans have to make sure they get plenty of protein from other sources. They must also make sure they get enough vitamins, especially B 12, and minerals such as iron, zinc, and calcium.

◀ Beans, lentils, and peas are a good source of protein and iron.

Good foods for vegetarians		
	sources	**more information**
protein	beans, peas and lentils; nuts and seeds; soya products; **quorn**; **textured vegetable protein**; milk, cheese and yoghurt; eggs	
vitamin B 12	soya products; fortified breakfast cereals; dairy products; eggs	some cereals and foods are fortified with B 12
iron	green leafy vegetables; dried fruit; pulses and seeds; fortified breakfast cereals	orange juice should be drunk with iron-rich foods (vitamin C helps the body absorb iron)
zinc	wholegrain bread; pulses, nuts and seeds; eggs	
calcium	spinach and broccoli; seeds and nuts; fortified soya products; dairy products	

EDWIN MOSES

US athlete Ed Moses dominated one of the world's toughest sports for ten years. As a vegetarian, he showed that you can certainly be super-fit and strong without eating meat. Moses burst onto the world scene when he won the gold medal in the 400-metre hurdles at the 1976 Olympics in Montreal. He won a second gold eight years later, in Los Angeles.

Moses improved the world record in his event four times. Between September 1977 and June 1987, he won 122 races, including 107 400-metre hurdles finals in a row! The wins included two World Championship golds and three World Cup titles. At the 1988 Olympics in Seoul, Moses won a bronze medal. This was the final race of his career.

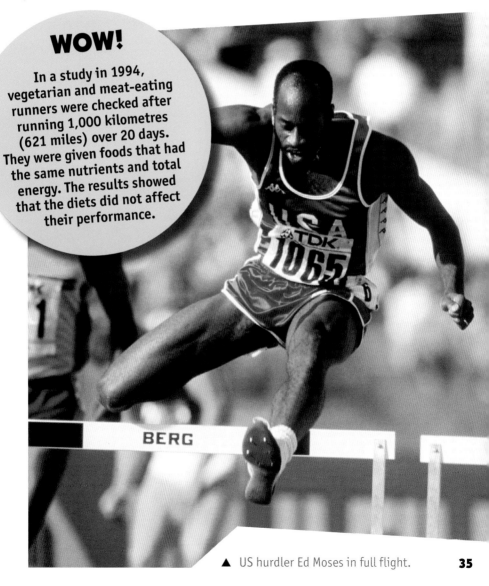

WOW!

In a study in 1994, vegetarian and meat-eating runners were checked after running 1,000 kilometres (621 miles) over 20 days. They were given foods that had the same nutrients and total energy. The results showed that the diets did not affect their performance.

▲ US hurdler Ed Moses in full flight.

TRAINING AND COMPETING
– eating to be fast

For young athletes and those who enjoy their sport at a social level, what they eat should stay the same most of the time. Even with a competition coming up, they should stick to their normal routine. This involves making sure that they eat a variety of foods every day and drink plenty of fluids so that they are well hydrated.

Top athletes may change their diet slightly when important competitions come around. But they always take training days seriously and use the same eating habits as they will during a big event. That way, there are no big surprises on competition day.

▶ Runners in training for a long-distance event.

LEADING UP TO A LONG RACE

Long-distance runners try to make sure that they are at their peak of health and fitness for their race. This includes having their energy levels at their highest. One of the most gruelling races is the marathon, which covers a distance of 42.2 kilometres (26 miles and 385 yards).

At least a week before the race, marathon runners eat plenty of foods that are rich in carbohydrate. They do this to top up their glycogen stores (see page 7) so that it will be as if they will have a full tank of fuel on the big day. During this week, runners eat lots of bread, rice, pasta, cereals, potatoes, fruit, and vegetables.

The day before the big race, runners eat as much carbohydrate as they can. However, they avoid wholegrain foods, because these take a long time to digest. They also avoid any food that they are not totally used to, because they want to avoid an upset stomach at all costs. Meals are topped up with high-carbohydrate snacks such as cereal bars.

ON THE DAY

Marathon runners have a meal (normally breakfast) two or three hours before the race. It is not good to run on an empty stomach. They choose foods that are high in carbohydrates, such as cereal, toast and jam, or pancakes. They drink a glass of fruit juice or a sports drink.

Again, there should be nothing new in the meal: top athletes practise their pre-race eating routine many times in training. Also, pre-race nerves play a part and make it difficult to eat too much.

During the race, runners grab a drink at the water stations. They drink little and often, to keep hydrated. In the major marathon races, there are usually drinks stations every mile (1.6 kilometres). Runners grab a plastic bottle, drink it on the run and then discard it at the side of the road.

Women's marathon

✔ In April 2003, British athlete Paula Radcliffe broke her own marathon world record by nearly 2 minutes, setting a new time of 2 hours, 15 minutes, and 25 seconds (2:15:25).

✔ Women have improved their long-distance times dramatically in recent years. The Olympic marathon was only introduced for women in 1984. The men's record of 2:04:55 was set in 2003 by Paul Tergat of Kenya. This is nearly 11 minutes faster than the women's record. Back in 1958, the fastest man was just 8 seconds quicker than the current women's record.

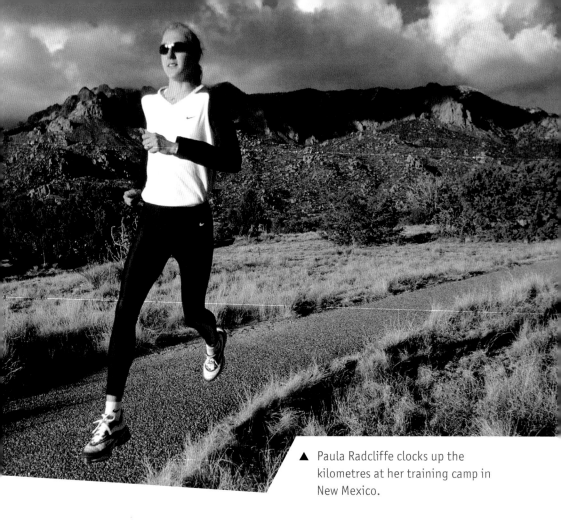

▲ Paula Radcliffe clocks up the kilometres at her training camp in New Mexico.

RADCLIFFE TREADING THIN LINE BETWEEN MARVEL AND COMIC

From what has been made public of her pre-race routine, Radcliffe gets up, has a bowl of porridge (scientists say its glycaemic index is low) and a sports drink (energy-boosting) before putting on her running kit (ultra-lightweight, heat-dispelling) [...] When it's over she has an ice bath (heals microscopic tears in muscle fibres), a massage (removes waste products and lactic acid from her legs), rubs on some emu oil (the elixir made from fatty tissue on the emu's back has potent healing properties), drinks a glass of bright green wheatgrass juice (full of nutrients), has a handful of vitamin supplements, eats some ostrich meat (low in fat, high in iron) and, finally one assumes, sits down.

The Guardian, 22 August 2005

You have to be at least 18 to run in a city marathon such as that of London, Boston, New York, or Sydney. Many cities organize half-marathons (21.1 km or 13.1 miles) – also for 18 years and over. There are also much shorter fun runs (a couple of kilometres) for younger athletes, in which children are welcome. In the London Marathon, there is a separate mini-marathon race for age groups 11–12, 13–14, and 15–17. It is run over the last 4.3 kilometres (2.7 miles) of the full marathon course.

If you are interested in running, as a serious sport or just for fun, get in touch with your local running club. An expert will make sure that you have fun learning to run the right distance at the right pace for your age and fitness.

AFTER THE EVENT

After competition, whether a long run or a game of tennis, the first aim is to build up energy again and make up for fluid losses. What you eat depends on whether you have finished for the day or have another event in a few hours' time. In any case, drinking is important, along with carbohydrate-rich foods such as pasta or baked potato. Rich or fatty foods should always be avoided.

▶ Tennis players have a short break at every changeover (after every two games). Here Venus Williams takes a drink of water at Wimbledon.

THE FASTEST PEOPLE ON EARTH

Who would you call the ultimate athletes? There are many candidates. Many people think the most amazing sportspeople are those who combine many events. Male and female triathletes swim, cycle, and run very long distances. Male decathletes compete in ten athletic events, and female heptathletes do seven.

At every Olympic Games and World Championship, the most popular spectator event is the 100-metre sprint. The winner of the men's event is often called the fastest human on earth. The current world record is 9.77 seconds, which means an average speed of 36.8 kilometres per hour (kph). That is nearly 23 miles per hour (mph). Back in 1896 the world's fastest sprinter managed 30 kph (19 mph). In the women's event, sprinters have improved by 2.3 seconds (6.2 kph or nearly 4 mph). How did sprinters gain that extra speed?

▼ Sprinters blast off their starting blocks at the 2004 Olympics in Athens.

Getting faster!

Some of the men's 100-m sprint world record holders 1896–2005		Some of the women's 100-m sprint world record holders 1922–2005	
12.0 Thomas Burke (US)	1896	12.8 Mary Lines (GB)	1922
11.0 Frank Jarvis (US)	1900	12.0 Betty Robinson (US)	1928
10.4 Charles Paddock (US)	1921	11.5 Helen Stephens (US)	1936
10.2 Jesse Owens (US)	1936	11.0 Wyomia Tyus (US)	1968
10.0 Armin Hary (West Germany)	1960	10.9 Renate Stecher (East Germany)	1973
9.90 Leroy Burrell (US)	1991	10.88 Marlies Oelsner (East Germany)	1977
9.86 Carl Lewis (US)	1991	10.87 Lyudmila Kondratyeva (USSR)	1980
9.84 Donovan Bailey (Canada)	1996	10.81 Marlies Göhr (East Germany)	1983
9.79 Maurice Greene (US)	1999	10.79 Evelyn Ashford (US)	1983
9.77 Asafa Powell (Jamaica)	2005	10.49 Florence Griffith-Joyner (US)	1988

Since 1988, five different male sprinters have improved the men's 100-m world record. During that time the women's record holder remained the same – Florence Griffith-Joyner (known as "Flo-Jo"), who died in 1998. She won three sprint gold medals at the 1988 Olympics, as well as one silver medal. She once said, "I trained a lot harder for the '88 Olympics. There is no substitute for hard work – I have the medals to prove it."

HOW TO GAIN SPEED

The main way to get faster is by using more modern training techniques. An important part of these is nutrition. Nutrition is the science of what you eat and how it affects your body. Getting their diet right helps sprinters train harder and longer. In turn, intense training helps them improve their fitness and technique so that they get faster.

Like all other athletes, sprinters choose a high-carbohydrate diet. This is especially useful for the quick, fast-burn energy they need. They also need great muscular power, which they build through weight-training. Sprinters need to be strong and muscular, but at the same time they require low body fat levels. Sprinters therefore look for low-fat foods.

Overall, a sprinter might take in up to three times as much energy (in calories) as an ordinary person. This might include a slightly higher proportion of carbohydrate, roughly the same proportion of protein, but a smaller percentage of fat.

SPRINTERS ON COMPETITION DAY

Sprinters have to be very careful with their diet on race days. Though each race lasts only seconds, they may have to run several heats and a final in one day. There is also a lot of waiting around in between. They normally start the day with a carbohydrate-based breakfast. Then they eat easily-digested snacks and drink lots of fluids during the day. Their aim is to not feel hungry, but at the same time not to have an uncomfortably full stomach.

Even faster?

✔ A mathematician might say that 200-metre runners are fastest! The world record is 19.32 seconds, set by Michael Johnson (US) in 1996. This works out to an average speed of 37.3 kph (23.2 mph). That is half a kph faster than the 100-m record. That's because a 200-metre runner starts the second 100 m of the race at full speed and does not have to accelerate twice.

✔ This is not the case with the women's records. Both were set by Florence Griffith-Joyner (known as "Flo-Jo") in 1988. Her 10.49 seconds for the 100 metre race (34.3 kph or 21.3 mph) is faster than her 21.34 seconds for the 200 (33.7 kph or 20.9 mph).

SCIENTISTS AND SPECIALISTS

Professional sportspeople rely on experts to help them make the right food choices for their very important diet. This is only possible because so much study and research have gone into what different foods contain and how they affect the human body. This research is carried out by food scientists and nutritionists.

▶ Food scientists carry out tests in a laboratory.

Dietitians are specially trained and qualified experts who help people with all aspects of nutrition and diet. Some dietitians specialize in sports, and they work with individual athletes, sports teams, and qualified coaches. They give advice on the best diet for particular sports and events. They may have a degree or diploma in sport dietetics.

Many top professional sportspeople have their own dietitian. They get advice on special diets for training and competition. Their health and performance are checked regularly to see that their personal nutrition programme is correct. Professional football teams also have their own diet experts to look after individual players.

▲ A specialist fitness coach guides players of the French national soccer squad, as they warm up for a training session.

CORNFLAKES OR PORRIDGE?

"Picture this: Morning of an Olympic distance triathlon, two hours before the race you are about to stock up on carbohydrate, what do you choose? Cornflakes or porridge? Choose cornflakes and feel that initial energy surge, but then potentially flagging energy resources in the later stages of the race. OR choose porridge and have a sustained and steadily released energy replenishment for the duration of the race. The choice is yours, but just thinking about thinking more carefully about the food you are eating could give you the edge you have been looking for."

Advice from British international triathlete Lisa Rowbottom

HEALTH PROBLEMS
– why a good diet is so important

Athletes on a good diet are less likely to have health problems. Sensible nutrition can help sportspeople avoid both illness and injury.

Food is important to all of us in terms of our general health. Proteins have a special role to play, because they help repair damaged cells. Minerals and vitamins are also vital to health. Some athletes take extra vitamins, such as vitamin C to fight colds, in the belief that they keep them healthy.

What causes a stitch?

✔ Have you ever suffered from a stitch in your side when running? Most people have. This annoying pain can often force runners to stop altogether. Some people think that a stitch is caused by eating or drinking too much just before setting out. This may be a factor.

✔ Scientific research has found a different cause for stitch, which sports scientists call ETAP (exercise-related transient abdominal pain). They believe that the pain is caused by a spasm or cramp in the abdominal muscle.

✔ Soccer and rugby players, swimmers and basketball players can also suffer from it. Fit athletes suffer less, which may be because they have a better breathing technique. Probably the best tips for avoiding stitch are – get fit and remember to breathe properly!

PROBLEMS WITH WEIGHT

Most athletes feel that they perform best at a certain weight. In some sports there are weight limits, which increase the pressure on athletes to watch their weight.

Many young people would like to be slimmer than they are. They might even be tempted to eat little and exercise a lot to try to get thinner. This is not a good idea.

If you are interested in long-distance sports such as running or cycling, or aesthetic sports such as gymnastics, figure skating, or diving, you might think it is important to be thin. However, the most important thing is to eat enough nourishing food to stay fit and healthy. Never try to lose weight drastically. This can lead to the development of an eating disorder, such as anorexia, which is very dangerous.

If you feel that you might have an eating or weight problem, or if you're just worried about your diet, it is important to ask for help. Speak at once to a parent or teacher, or another adult that you trust, and be honest with yourself and them. Disordered eating will not make you a better athlete and will certainly give you many other problems.

▲ US boxer Laila Ali poses during an official weigh-in in December 2005. Laila is the daughter of boxing legend Muhammad Ali.

PREVENTING AND HEALING INJURIES

The fitter an athlete is, the less likely he or she is to get injured. We also know that good nutrition is an important part of general fitness. Many sporting injuries are caused or made worse by tiredness. Surveys of both professional and holiday skiers, for example, show that they fall and hurt themselves more towards the end of a day on the slopes. This is because tiredness makes their brain less alert and their muscles less responsive.

▼ An injured soccer player is put on a stretcher and carried from the pitch.

Proteins, vitamins, and minerals (especially iron, zinc, and calcium) all play an important part in the healing process when a sportsperson is injured. Professional athletes may find that they need to reduce their energy intake when they are injured. This is because they cannot burn off as many calories when they are not training. This will not affect young sportspeople, who should always continue with their normal diet.

Full-time athletes can use time out caused by injury to plan for the future. They may look at their diet plan and decide how they might change things when they get back to full training.

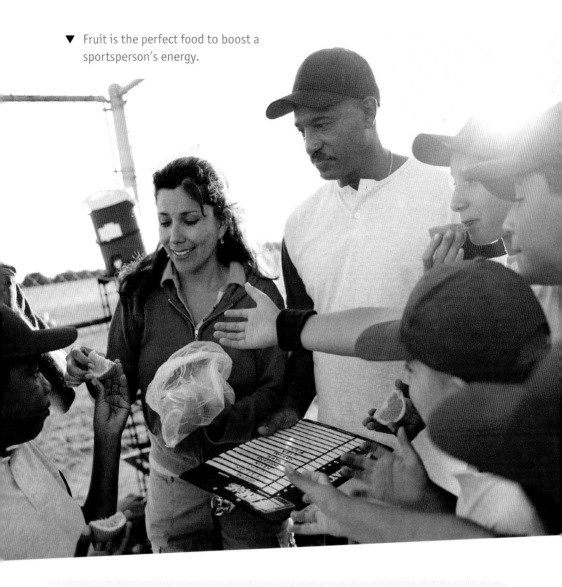

▼ Fruit is the perfect food to boost a sportsperson's energy.

Your balanced diet

Adult professional sportspeople may have special requirements for their particular activity. Some of them may take dietary supplements or eat an unusual mix of foods. You have read about some of these in this book. Remember that a growing young person's diet should always be varied and balanced. Your normal healthy diet will give you all the energy you need for your chosen sport.

SPORT AND FOOD FOR FUN

Sports are fun. They can help make you healthy and happy, and nutrition is a vital part of that. Though it's one of our most important basic needs, food can be fun too. You can enjoy your favourite meals and have special treats that form part of a healthy, balanced diet.

IDEAS FOR HEALTHY EATING

Here are some ideas to help you enjoy healthy food along with your sports. Forget about dieting or giving up things you love, but try to stick to a few rules. Eat a lot of fruit and vegetables. Make sure there is variety in your diet and avoid too many ready-prepared meals.

GRAB A SANDWICH!

Make a healthy, filling sandwich with thick slices of the following delicious breads:

- wholewheat
- rye
- sourdough
- sunflower-seed
- multi-grain
- three-seed
- ciabatta
- barley
- pitta.

▲ Low-fat natural yoghurt with strawberries is a great idea for when you are in a hurry.

SOME SUGGESTED SANDWICH FILLINGS

- hummus with lettuce and chopped peppers or grated carrot
- nut-butter with sliced banana
- tuna with watercress
- tomatoes, mozzarella, and salad leaves
- chopped chicken breast with rocket and sweetcorn
- guacamole (avocado with lemon juice and tomato)
- hard-boiled egg with reduced-fat mayonnaise
- Edam cheese, sliced apple, and lettuce
- Marmite (yeast and vegetable extract) with a thin slice of hard cheese and green salad leaves
- marinated tofu with shredded carrots and cabbage.

ON THE RUN

Here are some ideas for when you are in a hurry and need to grab something fast:

- fresh fruit (apple, banana, pear, grapes, clementine, plum, peach, etc.)
- low-fat fruit yoghurt
- fruit and cereal bar
- rice cakes and crackers
- wholemeal rolls, pitta bread, muffins, potato cakes, bagels filled with sliced banana, cottage cheese, peanut butter, olive spread
- breakfast cereal, muesli with semi-skimmed milk
- yoghurt drinks
- fruit juice.

A FEW MORE SUBSTANTIAL MEALS

- baked potato filled with baked beans, or olive spread and cheese
- mixed bean stew (with chickpeas, kidney beans, and butter beans)
- mixed vegetable stew (with courgettes, aubergines, tomatoes, and onions)
- pasta with different sauces (such as tomato, mushroom, broccoli, and peppers; or leeks, spinach, and asparagus, with a little grated cheese)
- vegetable stir-fries with tofu or cashew nuts
- chicken or beef stir-fries
- grilled white fish with potatoes and steamed vegetables.

▼ Pasta is fun and easy to cook.

RECIPES

STIR-FRIED CHICKEN WITH BEAN SPROUTS AND NOODLES

This meal is quick to make. It also combines a good source of protein with vitamins A, B, and C, as well as folic acid and iron. A round shallow pan, called a wok, allows you to use very little oil. If you do not have one, use a large non-stick frying pan. For a vegetarian stir-fry, add a handful of cashew nuts or chopped smoked tofu instead of chicken. When stir-frying, you have to stir the chicken and vegetables all the time.

Ingredients:
200 g boneless chicken breast, thinly sliced
2 tablespoons sunflower oil
150 g Chinese noodles
100 g bean sprouts
100 g sugar snap peas or mangetout, broken in half
1 carrot finely sliced
2 spring onions, roughly chopped
1 cm root ginger, peeled and grated (optional)
3 oyster or other mushrooms, thinly sliced
1 tablespoon dark soy sauce
1 tablespoon sesame seeds
1 clove garlic, crushed (optional)
juice of 1 orange
1 tablespoon flat-leaf parsley, chopped

Method:
Cook the noodles in boiling water for 3–4 minutes, according to packet instructions, and drain. Set them aside. Heat 1 tablespoon of oil in a wok, add the garlic and ginger, and cook for 10 seconds. Add the chicken, and stir-fry over high heat for 2 minutes, until the meat is cooked through. Stir in the sugar snaps and carrot, and fry for 2 minutes. Push to the side of the pan. Add the mushrooms, and stir-fry for a further 2 minutes. Put this mixture into a bowl. Heat the rest of the oil in the same wok and add the bean sprouts and onion. Stir-fry for 1–2 minutes. Season with soy sauce. Return the chicken and vegetable mixture to the wok, and stir in the orange juice and parsley. Reheat and mix well with the noodles. Cook for 2 minutes, until hot. Scatter with sesame seeds and serve at once.

▲ Vegetarian stir-fry with tofu instead of chicken

BERRY DELIGHT

Ingredients:

150 ml low-fat natural yoghurt
50–100 g berries (blueberries, raspberries, strawberries, redcurrants, or blackcurrants)
1 teaspoon honey
1 tablespoon pumpkin and sesame seeds.

Method:

To toast the seeds, first heat a heavy-based frying pan until hot. Put the seeds in and stir over a high heat, for about 1 minute. Leave to cool. Put the yoghurt in a bowl and stir in the berries. Sprinkle with seeds and enjoy!

▲ Berry delight

GLOSSARY

amino acid substance that occurs naturally in the body and forms proteins

balanced diet diet with the right amounts of different kinds of foods

calcium mineral that helps build strong bones

calorie unit of energy

carbohydrates starches and sugars, found in food, that are converted to glucose when they are digested. The glucose is used for energy.

cell smallest, microscopic part of a living thing

cereal grain seed from cereal plants such as maize, wheat, or rice

diet the kinds of food that a person usually eats

dietitian qualified expert who helps people with their diet and nutrition

digestion breaking down of food in the body

electrolytes mineral salts (such as sodium, potassium, and magnesium) that control the balance of fluids in the body

element chemical substance that cannot be broken down into a simpler substance

enzyme substance that speeds up chemical reactions in the body

essential fatty acid type of acid found in fat that the body needs

fibre substance in plants that cannot be digested, but which helps people to digest food

glucose simple form of sugar found in many carbohydrates

glycaemic index (**GI**) system of numbers that shows how fast individual foods affect blood sugar after they have been eaten

glycogen substance stored in the muscles that changes to glucose and gives energy

hormone natural substance that regulates bodily processes

hydrated having enough water in the body

kilocalorie (kcal) unit of energy (equal to a thousand calories, or 4.18 kilojoules)

kilojoule (kJ) unit of energy (equal to a thousand joules, or 0.24 kilocalories)

lentil seed of a plant of the pea family

macronutrients substances in food (nutrients) that we need in large amounts – carbohydrates, proteins, and fats

maize cereal plant (also called corn) that is grown for its grain

micronutrients substances in food (nutrients) that we need in small amounts – vitamins and minerals

millet cereal plant that is grown for its grain

mineral chemical substance that occurs naturally in the soil and in foods. We need certain minerals in small quantities to be healthy.

molecule simple unit of a chemical substance

oats cereal plant that is grown for its grain

omega-3 fatty acid type of unsaturated fat mainly found in oily fish

organ part inside the body that has a special job to do

protein natural substance made up of amino acids that is needed for strength and growth

pulses seeds of plants such as peas, beans, and lentils

quorn vegetarian food made by fermenting the fungus *Fusarium gramineurum*. It is then flavoured and shaped.

saturated fats fats found in meat and animal products

supplement substance added to a person's diet, usually in the form of tablets

textured vegetable protein defatted soya flour that has been processed and flavoured so that it resembles meat

tissue body material made up of cells

tofu vegetarian food used in China and Japan made from soya milk. Also known as bean curd or soya cheese.

unsaturated fat fat that has few hydrogen atoms

urine fluid made up of waste products that is stored in the bladder and released when a person goes to the toilet

vitamins group of substances we need to be healthy

wholegrain cereal grain that did not have the bran and embryo removed when it was processed

FINDING OUT MORE

BOOKS

Body Needs: titles include *Vitamins and minerals for a healthy body,*
Carbohydrates for a healthy body, Fats for a healthy body, and *Water and*
fibre for a healthy body (Heinemann Library, 2003). This series looks at
what the human body needs to function healthily.

Complete Guide to Sports Nutrition, Anita Bean (Black, 2003)

Encyclopedia of World Sport, David Levinson and Karen Christensen
(ABC-CLIO, 1996)

Just the Facts: Drugs and Sport, Clive Gifford (Heinemann Library, 2003)

Making of a Champion: titles include *A World-Class Mountain Biker,*
A World-Class Gymnast, and *A World-Class Sprinter*
(Heinemann Library, 2004)

Teen issues: Fitness and *Diet*, Joanna Kedge and Joanna Watson
(Raintree, 2004)

The Olympics: titles include *Great Olympic Moments* and *Modern*
Olympics, Haydn Middleton (Heinemann Library, 2000)

Trends in Food Technology: titles include *The Food Industry, Safe Food,*
Food Processing, and *Food Ingredients* (Heinemann Library, 2005).

Understanding Ingredients, Anne Barnett (Heinemann Library, 1998)

FURTHER RESEARCH

If you are interested in finding out more about sports or nutrition, try
researching the following topics:

- the training and preparation needed to become a world-class athlete
- the history of the Olympics, including the ancient Games at Olympia
  and the Modern Games since 1896
- how sportspeople are tested for drugs, and the banned substances
  they need to avoid
- fitness and diet for individual sports (governing bodies of sports
  usually give advice on their websites)
- preparing for winter sports (and especially the Winter Olympics).

WEBSITES

www.defra.gov.uk

UK Department for Environment, Food and Rural Affairs (Defra) aims to "work for the essentials of life – food, air, land, water, people, animals, and plants".

www.food.gov.uk

The main website of the Food Standards Agency (FSA), an independent UK government department.

www.eatwell.gov.uk

An FSA website that provides consumer advice and information on healthy eating.

www.affa.gov.au

The Australian Department of Agriculture, Fisheries, and Forestry website.

www.uksport.gov.uk

National sports organization in the United Kingdom that aims to lead UK sports to world-class success.

www.ausport.gov.au

The website of the Australian Sports Commission. This body aims to coordinate the Government's commitment and contribution to sport.

www.edauk.com

This is the website of the UK Eating Disorders Association which provides information and help on all kinds of eating disorders.

www.eda.org.au

The website of the Australian Eating Disorders Association.

www.foodstandards.gov.au

Food labels differ around the world; this site contains useful information about food labels from Australia and New Zealand.

www.iaaf.org

International Association of Athletics Federations (IAAF) has lots of information if you want to research world records and rankings, etc.

www.olympic.org

This is the official website of the Olympic Movement. It has links to all the international sports federations.

INDEX

adrenaline 15
alcohol 29
amino acids 14, 16

Body Mass Index 31
body shapes 30
body tissue 5, 15, 30
brain 10, 46

calories 6, 9, 13
carbohydrates 8, 9,
  10–13, 29, 37, 39, 41
  complex 10
  simple 10, 11
cramps 24, 25, 28, 44

dehydration 28–29
diet 5, 9, 24, 32, 47
  weight-loss diet 32
dietitians 16, 43
digestion 9, 37

eating disorder 33, 44,
  45
electrolytes 29
endurance sports 17
energy 4, 6, 11, 41
  stores 7, 11
enzymes 15

fat(s)
  body fat 7, 19, 20,
    30
  dietary fats 8–9,
    18–21, 41
  fatty acids 18, 24
  saturated fats 18, 20
  unsaturated fats 18

fibre 9
fluids 9, 26–29, 37, 39
food labels 8
fruit and vegetables 9,
  22, 23, 47

glucose 10, 11, 29
glycaemic index (GI)
  12
glycogen 7, 11, 37
gymnastics 32–33

health problems 44–47
hormones 15

kilojoules (kJ) 6

long-distance running
  28, 36, 37–39

marathons 37, 39
meat and fish 9, 16, 23
milk and dairy
  products 9, 16, 23
muscles 4, 7, 11, 15,
  19, 24, 25, 30, 33,
  41, 46

nutrients 8–9
  macro- 8, 9, 14
  micro- 8, 22
nutritionists 42
nuts 14, 16

overhydration 29
oxygen 4, 23

pee charts 27

performance-
  enhancing drugs 25
protein 8, 9, 14–17, 34,
  41, 44, 46
pulses 9, 16, 23

Radcliffe, Paula 37, 38
recipes
  berry delight 51
  meal ideas 49
  sandwich fillings 48
  snacks 49
  stir-fried chicken 50

soya products 9, 16
sports drinks 13, 29, 37
sprinting 40–42
starches 9, 10, 11
stitch 44
strength/power sports
  17
sugars 10, 11
sumo wrestling 20–21
sweating 26, 27, 28

Tour de France 12, 13

vegans 34
vegetarians 16, 34, 35
vitamins and minerals
  9, 22–25, 44, 46
  supplements 24, 25

water 9, 26–28, 37, 39
weight fluctuations 32
weight problems
  44–45
wholegrain foods 37
wrestling 17